KIDS ASK ABOUT
FARM ANIMALS

WHAT are horses called?

WHY are farm animals important?

DO pigs have good senses?

Written by Joanna Jarc Robinson
Illustrated by Cindy Kiernicki

sequoia kids media

Visit us at SequoiaKidsMedia.com for bonus downloadable content

Photography © Shutterstock 2022 AB Photographie; Africa Studio; Arteach1;
Steve Boice; conrado; Mircea Costina; Linn Currie; cynoclub; DenisNata; Enna8982; gabriel12; Eric Isselee;
JIANG HONGYAN; I Wei Huang; imagesbycat; huang jenhung; Dmytro Khlystun; Kwadrat; Erik Lam;
Ievgenii Meyer; liskus; lovelyday12; LP Design; Dudarev Mikhail; Monkey Business Images;
Aksenova Natalya; New Africa; Simone Padovani; photomaster; seeshooteatrepeat;
Elena Sherengovskaya; simpleman; Tammy27; Juice Verve; vvg42; 2009fotofriends

Published by Sequoia Kids Media,
an imprint of Sequoia Publishing & Media, LLC

Sequoia Publishing & Media, LLC,
a division of Phoenix International Publications, Inc.

8501 West Higgins Road, Chicago, Illinois 60631
34 Seymour Street, London W1H 7JE
Heimhuder Straße 81, 20148 Hamburg

© 2023 Sequoia Publishing & Media, LLC
First Published © 2023 Twin Sisters IP, LLC. All rights reserved.

Customer Service: CS@SequoiaKidsBooks.com

Sequoia Kids Media and associated logo are trademarks and/or registered trademarks of
Sequoia Publishing & Media, LLC.

Active Minds is a registered trademark of Phoenix International Publications, Inc.
and is used with permission.

All rights reserved. This publication may not be reproduced in whole or
in part by any means without permission from the copyright owners.
Permission is never granted for commercial purposes.

This book is sold subject to the condition that it shall not, by way of trade or otherwise,
be lent, resold, hired out, or otherwise circulated without the publisher's prior consent in
any form or binding or cover other than that in which it is published and without similar
condition being imposed on the subsequent purchaser.

www.SequoiaKidsMedia.com

Library of Congress Control Number: 2022920278

ISBN: 979-8-7654-0175-0

KIDS ASK ABOUT

FARM ANIMALS

TABLE OF CONTENTS

Why are farm animals important? What do pigs eat?	4
Who are the members of pig families?	5
Do pigs have good senses?	6
Who are cows?	8
How many types of chickens are there?	10
What do chickens look like?	11
Who are goats?	12
What do goats look like?	13
Who are sheep? What are sheep covered in?	14
What are horses called?	16
What do horses do?	18
What other birds might be found on farms? Where do ducks and geese live?	20
What do ducks and geese eat?	21
What are turkeys called? What do male turkeys look like?	22

PIGS

WHY are farm animals important?

Farm animals help us in many ways! They provide lots of different services both on and off farms as well as useful products. Caring for farm animals is hard work, but learning how teaches valuable life skills like confidence and responsibility. Whether you live on a farm or in the city, there are plenty of ways to interact with and learn from farm animals!

Sow

Piglets

WHAT do pigs eat?

Pigs eat plants or animals, like corn, potatoes, grains, grass, eggs, frogs, snakes, and fish.

WHO are the members of pig families?

Mother pigs are called sows, father pigs are called boars, and baby pigs are called piglets. A sow usually gives birth to 8–12 piglets at a time. A whole group of pigs is called a herd.

DID YOU KNOW?

Pigs are sensitive to the sun and don't have any sweat glands, so they roll in the mud to keep cool.

DO pigs have good senses?

Pigs have poor eyesight, but they have a highly developed sense of smell. They are used by some police departments to sniff out drugs.

Miniature pig

IT'S A FACT!

The smallest pig is the miniature pig, standing 15 to 20 inches (38–50 centimeters) tall and weighing 50 to 150 pounds (23–68 kilograms). The largest pig is the giant forest hog which weighs 600 pounds (272 kg) and stands 3 feet (0.9 meter) tall!

Giant forest hog

PIGS PROVIDE:
- Pork
- Gelatin
- Medicine
- Leather
- Paintbrush bristles

COWS

WHO are cows?

Cows are some of the largest farm animals. They eat a lot of corn, grass from the pasture, and hay. Cows must be mothers before they can produce milk. Female cows who have not yet given birth are called heifers. Male cows are known as bulls. Baby cows are called calves. A whole group of cows is called cattle.

Holstein cow

IT'S A FACT!

Cows usually live for about 6 or 7 years, but they can live up to 25 years.

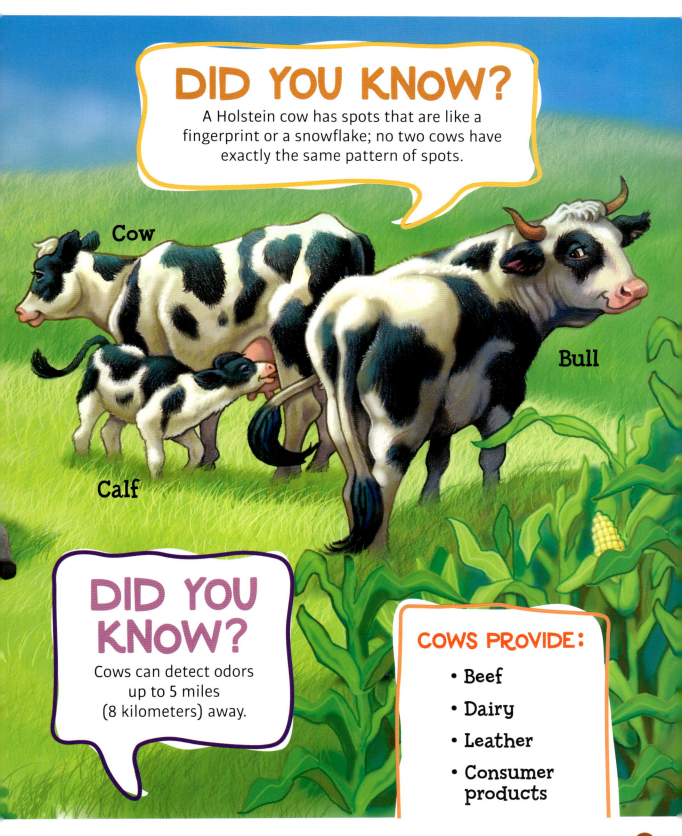

DID YOU KNOW?

A Holstein cow has spots that are like a fingerprint or a snowflake; no two cows have exactly the same pattern of spots.

Cow

Bull

Calf

DID YOU KNOW?

Cows can detect odors up to 5 miles (8 kilometers) away.

COWS PROVIDE:

- Beef
- Dairy
- Leather
- Consumer products

CHICKENS

HOW many types of chickens are there?

There are over 150 different breeds, sizes, and colors of chickens. A group of chickens is called a flock.

DID YOU KNOW?

Most chickens can't fly! Instead, their feathers help protect them from getting too cold or wet.

CHICKENS PROVIDE:
- Eggs
- Poultry
- Medicine

WHAT do chickens look like?

Chickens have growths called combs on top of their heads and wattles under their chins to help keep their bodies cool in the heat.

Comb

Wattle

IT'S A FACT!

Chickens have a well-developed gizzard (a part of the stomach that contains tiny stones) to grind up their food.

GOATS

GOATS PROVIDE:
- Milk
- Meat
- Wool
- Leather

Doe or nanny

Kid

WHO are goats?

Female goats are called does or nannies while male goats are known as bucks or billies. Baby goats are called kids. Goats eat corn, oats, hay, grass, alfalfa, and weeds. They have excellent night vision and can run, climb, and jump over 5 feet high. They can even stand on their back legs to reach tree branches!

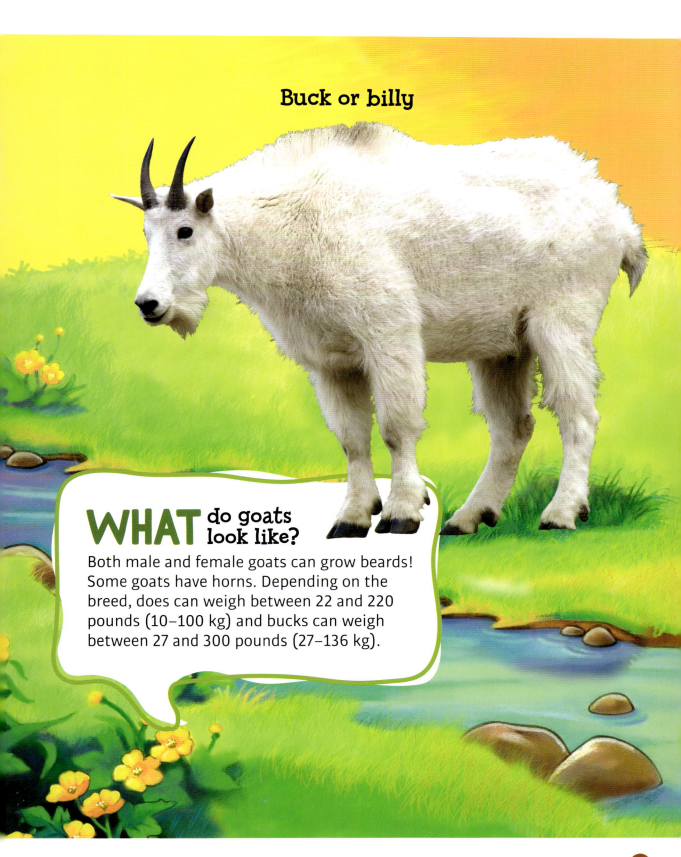

Buck or billy

WHAT do goats look like?

Both male and female goats can grow beards! Some goats have horns. Depending on the breed, does can weigh between 22 and 220 pounds (10–100 kg) and bucks can weigh between 27 and 300 pounds (27–136 kg).

SHEEP

WHO are sheep?

There are more than 200 breeds of domesticated sheep. Male sheep are called rams, females are ewes, and babies are lambs. They move in large groups called flocks. Sheep have poor eyesight, but an excellent sense of hearing. Lambs know their mother by her bleat, or the sound she makes.

WHAT are sheep covered in?

Sheep have a thick coat of wool on their body. This coat is called a fleece. Sheep wool is used in clothing like sweaters, mittens, and pants. Wool is fire-resistant and will not burn.

HORSES

WHAT are horses called?

Baby horses are called foals—male baby horses are colts and female babies are fillies. Adult male horses who can breed are known as stallions while females are called mares. A group of horses is called a herd. Ponies are small horses.

Stallion

Colt

Mare

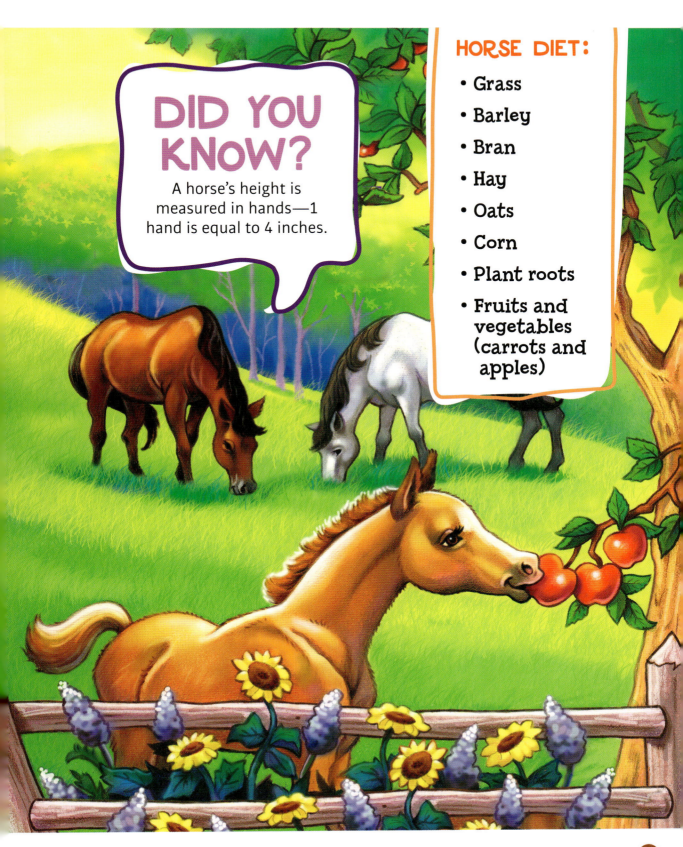

DID YOU KNOW?

A horse's height is measured in hands—1 hand is equal to 4 inches.

HORSE DIET:

- Grass
- Barley
- Bran
- Hay
- Oats
- Corn
- Plant roots
- Fruits and vegetables (carrots and apples)

WHAT do horses do?

Horses do many things on the farm. They can walk, trot, canter (a jogging or running pace), and gallop. Horses are also very strong and can pull heavy loads like wagons and plows.

DID YOU KNOW?

Horses are also used for entertainment! People can ride on their backs for fun or watch them run in horse races.

BIRDS

WHAT other birds might be found on farms?

Ducks, geese, and turkeys can be found on farms. Adult female ducks are called hens and adult male ducks are drakes. Baby ducks are known as ducklings while baby geese are goslings. Both birds molt, which means the adults shed their old feathers to make way for new ones. They also migrate, or travel to warm places for the winter.

Goose

Goslings

GEESE PROVIDE:

- Poultry
- Eggs
- Feathers for bedding and clothing

WHERE do ducks and geese live?

Geese and ducks are types of waterfowl, which are aquatic birds that live on or near bodies of water like ponds, rivers, and lakes. They have webbed feet, which are like paddles to help them swim.

DUCKS PROVIDE:
- Poultry
- Eggs
- Feathers for bedding
- Oils for soap

Drake

Ducklings

Hen

WHAT do ducks and geese eat?

Ducks and geese both eat plants—like grass. Geese also eat slugs, snails, worms, and baby rats. In addition to plants, ducks eat insects, snails, fish, and seeds.

WHAT are turkeys called?

Adult female turkeys are called hens, like ducks and chickens. Adult male turkeys are called toms. A group of adult turkeys is called a rafter. Baby turkeys are called poults, and they live in groups called broods.

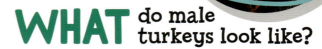

WHAT do male turkeys look like?

Toms have long wattles—brightly colored skin that hangs from their necks. They are also more colorful than hens.

TURKEYS PROVIDE:

- Poultry
- Consumer products

DID YOU KNOW?

Turkeys feed on insects, plants, corn, wheat, and seeds. They do not like water. Mother turkeys can lay about 9–18 eggs in clutches (sets or clusters of eggs) in nests made of dried leaves and grasses.

IT'S A FACT!

Wild turkeys can fly, and they roost (or sleep) in trees.

FARM ANIMALS ARE AMAZING!

They help make lots of different products for people. People need to respect and help farm animals by making sure that they have plenty of food and water, a clean and safe place to live, and a healthy life that is free from disease.

Some people have formed groups that help protect farm animals from cruel treatment, stress, pain, and unhealthy slaughter. These groups also help to protect people and the environment from chemicals used on factory farms.